Holly Celebrates Earth Day

Written by Kimberly Kendall-Drucker

Holly Celebrates Earth Day

Copyright © 2022. Kimberly Kendall-Drucker All rights reserved. No portion of this book may be reproduced in any form without expressed written permission from Just Write Publications or Kimberly Kendall-Drucker except as permitted by U.S. copyright law.

No part of this publication may be reproduced, stored in a retrieval system, or transmitted in any form or by any means, electronic, mechanical, photocopied, recorded, or otherwise, without written permission from the author. For information regarding permission, visit kimberlykendalldrucker.com.

Library of Congress Control Number: 2022901683

Hardback ISBN: 978-0-578-36393-6

Paperback ISBN: 978-0-578-37952-4

To Mommy – my Best Girl, Levones Chisholm
Thank you for teaching me the importance of leaving the planet better than I found it. You are the best mother on Earth. I love you.

To my beloved husband Larry, for whom every day is indeed Earth Day
Thank you for your commitment to recycling and working to reduce our carbon footprint. You drive an EV and are dedicated to preserving our resources and loving our planet.
I see solar panels in our future.
You are my favorite husband on Earth. I love you.

For my Beautiful Busy
I look forward to seeing you make your mark on the planet.
You are a perfect Holly and a marvelous niece. I am grateful. I love you.

For my darling nephew, Sincere
You were born almost 11 years ago – just a day after Earth Day. You have been making the planet a better place ever since. I love you.

For my father, Humphrey Kendall
Among my most treasured childhood memories are the walks you, Ishmael, and I took along the Eno River - talking, laughing, and picking up trash along the way. You are my favorite scientist on Earth – next to Neil DeGrasse Tyson. 😄 I love you.

Holidays are happy days.
They happen all year-through.
Some holidays look at the past -
For some we start brand new.

There are Holly-Days of service
Holly-Days for being jolly,
And I celebrate each one of them
Because my name is Holly.

APRIL

S	M	T	W	T	F	S
					1	2
3	4	5	6	7	8	9
10	11	12	13	14	15	16
17	18	19	20	21	22	23
24	25	26	27	28	29	30

Every April 22nd
People gather everywhere.
We help to beautify our planet.
We show the Earth how much we care.

But Earth Day should be everyday
Each day. Each month. Each year.
To love our planet and to treat it well —
Because we all live here.

Our planet is incredible.
She's green and blue and vast.
Each continent is **magical**
From the first one to the last.

AFRICA

African Grasslands – great and gold
Where Lions and Zebras roam
Wild Giraffes, Gazelles, and Starlings
All call these Savannas home.

AUSTRALIA

Australia is the land down under
Filled with Eucalyptus Trees,
Koala Bears and swampy wetlands
Kangaroos and Wallabies.

Europe
Asia

Although **Europe** seems quite fancy,
There is lots of wildlife there.
In the snowy Alpine Mountains -
Live the Ibex, Wolf, and Hare.

In the **Asian** Himalayas
You see Red Pandas and more -
Rhinos, Yaks, and Bengal Tigers,
Snow Leopards and even Boar.

North America

North America has Buffalo
And Moose and Caribou,
Mountain Lions, Beavers, Canada Geese
Ducks, and Bald Eagles too!

South America

South America's Rainforest
Is the most biodiverse.
More plants and animals are living there -
Than any place on earth.

Pale Pink Dolphins and Black Monkeys
See-thru green Glass Frogs and more -
Half the animals on our planet
Make their home on the Amazon floor.

Antarctica

Antarctica is a frozen land
With mountains, lakes, and rivers.
Penguins lounge about atop sea ice
Where we'd all get the shivers.

But the sea ice is now **melting**.
Climate change is on the rise –
And the earth's natural resources
Are withering before our eyes.

We must stop filling all our landfills
With so much single-use plastic
Because our planet is in danger
If we don't do something drastic.

My friends and family made a pledge.
I made a promise too -
To be much kinder to our planet
For we have so much work to do.

Now, my family carries refuse bags
When we take a walk each day.
We pick up litter and recycling
We find flung along the way.

If we throw all our recyclables
Into the big blue bins
We can cut down on the loads of trash
And everybody wins.

When I go to the store with Mommy
I carry bags we can reuse,
And when they ask paper or plastic
I don't even have to choose.

Mommy says sustainability
Is what it's all about.
When we reduce, reuse, recycle
We can help our planet out!

When my "cuz" Sincere buys soda pop
He cuts the plastic rings

So, they do not harm the turtles
Or hurt other ocean beings.

Sincere rounded up his brothers,
And we planted blooming trees.
We even planted a bee garden
To help the butterflies and bees.

Even though we're only little kids
We surely understand it.
We know just how serious it is.
We can help save our planet.

We must ALL protect our oceans.
We must ALL protect our lands.
My teacher said for kids like us -
The future is in our hands.

We are all in this together.
Me and you and you and me
We must take care of this great planet
Because there is no Planet B!

If everyone just does their part
To help along the way,
Then our Mother Earth will flourish -
And **every day** will be **Earth Day**.

The End

Next in the Series...

Holly Celebrates Juneteenth

Holly Celebrates Independence Day

About the Author

Kimberly Kendall-Drucker lives in Charlotte, North Carolina with her husband Larry and Persian kitty, Zuzu. She loves reading, and her books are her friends. Her favorite childhood books are *Where the Sidewalk Ends, Roll of Thunder Hear My Cry, A Wrinkle in Time,* and *Are You There, God? It's Me Margaret*. Kimberly reads a book a week – sometimes two. She is committed to writing accessible books children enjoy - because readers are leaders.

Kimberly loves Phase 10, macaroni and cheese, the Oxford Comma, and graphic tees. She is currently obsessed with Wordle. Jeopardy is her favorite TV show. While some people are outdoorsy, Kimberly is decidedly indoorsy. Still, she loves a day at the beach. For Kimberly, family is everything, and her nieces and nephews are her pride and joy.

Holly Celebrates Earth Day is the third book in the *Holly Celebrates Series* and is Kimberly's fourth children's book.

To contact Kimberly or learn more about her, check out her website – **kimberlykendalldrucker.com**.

www.ingramcontent.com/pod-product-compliance
Lightning Source LLC
Chambersburg PA
CBHW041200290426
44109CB00002B/79